M000248568

EMOTIONAL RESIDUE
June 12, 2020
Copyright © 2020 Teeality
Written by "Teeality."
www.TeealityMusic.com
Gone Wit it Entertainment

"The most beautiful people we have known are those who have known defeat, known suffering, known struggle, known loss, and have found their way out of the depths. These persons have an appreciation, a sensitivity, and an understanding of life that fills them with compassion, gentleness, and a deep loving concern."

- Elizabeth Kübler-Ross

Dedicated to the woman that never allows me to down play myself.

J.W

Experience is the byproduct of vulnerability and love. Poetry is the reward hidden in healing and growing. Whether it's standing in puddles of your tears or spitting confetti from your smiles, I'll always be here.

Residue #6122020

I just want to say I love you all!
Hope everyone is growing towards the best
version of yourself.
Hope every ailment in your body is
dissolving.
Courage is no longer dormant in your body.
I hope your mathematics is improving and
you are calculating your worth correctly.
Every childhood wound is healing.
Every bad relationship experience is proving
to be necessary to get you to your true life
partner. 3rd eye opening and you see a
different world begging for a different you.
Families break cycles and let go of traditions
that have done more destruction than
restructuring to the youth and elders.
May positive thoughts invade your mind so
that you can manifest everything that you
desire. The world is abundant, enough for
everyone.
No need to envy or steal. I've heard so many
times "so and so would be turning in their
graves" ... it doesn't look like there's enough
room in coffins for the dead to roll over.
So, let's have more consideration for those
that are not in coffins, the living.
Let's treat the living better than we have
before perhaps better than we should.
All generations need new energy.
I offer everyone good energy. Know that you
are loved.... genuinely... and that's ok.

Even if it's not what you're use to... even if
you've forgotten how it feels.
YOU ARE LOVED.
I love you all and appreciate you.

#2006

It's like the ink in my pen says
"Take your time Tee, I'll help you" And my
paper says
"Everything you ever wrote, I felt you"

Residue #424

Why do pretty girls have the most tears
Even with a million compliments in both ears
Cast on their broken hearts
Covered with "I was here" signatures
Strings attached to the open parts
Because even body language needs a listener
Tensed necks need soft lips
Imagination needs options
Thighs need firm grips
Even if someone doesn't want to fully enter
Feels good to hear someone knocking
Means that they acknowledge someone is
home
Yet the emptiness inside of pretty girls is
always a reminder
That someone is gone

Residue #1217
When we become adults
We use real people as temporary band-aids

Residue #305
Saving driftwood we write poems in the sand
of sunless oceans
Hopeless romantics or romantics hoping
New moons will bring new waves
Bae watching which life to save

Residue #904
The new me.. Appreciates the old you
I often wonder if someday......we can make
the old.....new
So that I can give you all of the love that I
owe you
Sincerely
Oh, If only you knew
How much I do
Do Love You

Residue #308
Do you think about me
Early in the morning before the sun can even
rise
Do you dream about me
I have these feelings that I can't keep inside
I wined and dined you
I wined and dined you
But you couldn't see
Everything you had in me

Oh, I could drown a million times
But you would never want to be mine, no
I could cry a million times
But still you wouldn't be mine
Another page in my diary
Are you even sorry
Anybody knows me knows I'm a sucker for
love
You took advantage, yea
I don't understand it
Where do I go from here
How do I live
I could cry a million times
And you would still never be mine

Residue #222
So I'm in this relationship pretending not to
be strong
Because dealing with this sh** helps me to
write songs
I like you then I hate you
I write you then I play you

Residue #129
Most people think survival mode is bad, it's
actually not
But being on constant defense can be pretty
tiring
Evacuating hostile environments can change
everything

Residue #215
Unfortunately...I'm Right where you don't
want me
Triple entendre

Residue #522
Our last kiss
Your lips
Taste like envelope glue I knew
Still I didn't ask for a tracking number

Residue #411
Still in Love
Still in love Hey
Little darling
I'm still in love yea
Still in love
Little darling
I'm still in love
Good at your lying
Good at your trying
Good dutty wine
So I'm not good with goodbye, no
Adjust your vibe
Give me some time
Get out my mind
Get out of my soul
How could I, be willing to do anything for
you
When the tears from my eyes could never
ever afford you
Since you've been gone I vibrate higher
And I can have anyone that I desire

I said Since you've been gone I vibrate higher
And I can have anyone that I desire
But I'm still in love...
Little darling
I'm still in love
(Little darling I'm still in love with you)
Still in love
Little darling
(Little darling I'm still in love with you)
I'm still in love, hey
Little darling I'm still in love with you
Adjust your vibes
Good dutty wining
Adjust your vibes

Residue #120
I tend to love without attachment
Subconscious re-enactments
Of qualities my parent's relationship lacked in

Residue #116
Same way you trust amazon your package is
on the way
Same way you have to trust universe package
on the way

Residue #131
There's two kinds of love
The kind that submits and the kind that
haunts us

Residue #206
I'll never play with your mind because that's
how you make a living
I'll never break your heart because it has to
love our children
I will keep tears from your eyes hopefully it
will keep me in your vision
I attach my ears to your soul committing to
listen
Your every want, your every need I give my
undivided attention
For as long as I'm living

Residue #209
Your name is my haiku
Search if you like never will find someone
That loves you like I do

Residue #305
I don't mind being the only one naked
If you promise to keep me coming
Spiritually and emotionally in the healthiest
way
I don't mind investing my time, my attention,
my trust
If you build a home for my energy where the
wealthiest stay
Those rich in honesty, rich in loyalty
Rich in faithfulness, I'll easily give you more
of me
I don't mind my heart's beat being the loudest

in the room until yours can match its rate
I'll let you soak my sleeves with your
abandoned colored tears from a love that
refused to stay I'll get under you until you can
get over it, build you up
I'll water you, water me until we fill the cup
Grow, heal, flow
Spill love all over our dehydrated parts

Residue #908
We must do something about those who do
nothing
Eye see, eye know, eye grow

Residue #1210
Time will show you one of two things
Yes, he or she was bulls**ing
Or that you were and is the one who's
bulls**ing
Dispositional attribution awareness

Residue #1125
May your creations predict your success
So that predicaments never limit your success

Residue #1118
Poetry is the possibility of language
We are the possibility of love
I love me, I love you..I love us..we love
Our love is unworldly
It resides where souls collide
Where lies hide
It's a love to which angels subscribe

If I had known years ago what your love
would provide
Well I did know...and that's why I'm still by
your side
There's something about you
That makes me believe in you
And me

Residue #421
I will never forgive your lips for the way they
separated from mine
Causing my heartbeat to lose time
Offering no CPR forcing my body, mind, and
soul to realize that we
We are not what we think we are
An internal battle poisoned by a snake with a
silent rattle

Residue #805
If only you had grown tired of faking
Before I grew tired of waiting

Residue #122
Compatible with your birth sign
Made me adaptable to the worst signs
And red flags
Bed and bath
F*** up my head math
Sent love letters that should have stayed
drafts
Cried over things when I should have laughed
Lowered myself even thou
I knew you were all cap

I'm deep poetry deserving of all snaps
Now when you're present you gets no Rap

Residue #307
I never wanted to block your number, I loved
you, did you love me
Often times I stopped to wonder
I prayed god would keep me from the battles
in me
I blindly compromised yet you convinced me
that it was our compatibility
I kept my heart outrageously open for your
convenience
Your heart had guards and was closed in
How inconvenient for someone ready for
love
Willing to trust
A situation that had yet to prove its worth
An empty designer purse
Value measured by the visual beauty, yea you
look good
Did you notice how I got quiet, the length of
my silence
The change in my diet, the strength of my
crying
Did you see how burdens restructured my
posture
When you asked if I was unhappy, my mouth
said "no"
You didn't recognize the imposter
You never realized that I was no longer me
Because you were no longer peace

Residue #121

There are things I don't want to know
And things that you don't want to have to
answer
We don't want the side effects of the chemo
So we suffer with the cancer
Seasons change the color of leaves as if
they're our mood rings
Distant emotionally but you stay close to me
just to see the name that pops up when my
phone rings Every time I wish it was the old
you calling me
I gave the old you all of me
Maybe that's why I'm not enough for this
new you
When you said jump I landed on the moon
Loved you the whole way back too
I gave you space still for me you had no room
Standing outside, I wondered what did I come
back to

Residue #909

Sitting in my car reading the Bible
Seems I only talk to god in times of survival

Residue #215

At one time... the vending machine was the
only thing
That I could afford on an empty stomach
I appreciate CHANGE
Focused for it.. numbers blocked for it
Folks cut off for it

Residue #1129

Fearless so the truth is easily spoken
Check the notebooks I wrote in
Ink smeared from tears soaked in, years of
hoping
Through ears I'm coping
Hard to understand the game and be a good
sport when
Witnessing your mom giving other kids
support
Like damn where's my presents
Why am I present
Would have already offed myself but music is
a blessing
Its over everything, relationships, kids, and
wedding rings, no trophies or lettermans
Could have definitely dealt with better men
On this road to success
We done came a long way, many days it
seemed like the wrong way
But looking back it was the strong way
Lost our versions of Pac and Biggie, with
Leck and Jae city
The memory Lays on my shoulder a big F**
you to my city
Because we never did it for the fame
Y'all derailed the last train
Out of Paris

Residue #723
All these side hustles I juggle to avoid "the struggle"
These goals require soul muscle

Residue #206
Where are the words when I'm with you
Speechless

Residue #316
You can have anyone you want
You have mind control over others
You can also have anything you want
It's still mind control

Residue #603
Last night we did some things that you've never done
Keep the secret between you, me, and the sun

Residue #1228
I want real love....love that doesn't have hurt involved
A love evolved
That laying on your stomach listening to our baby's heartbeat Love
That replacing old fast food bags in the backseat with a baby car seat
 Love A love that loves no company
So misery knows not to come for me...Love
Love that remembers your scent from the

first day that we met
Nose still wide open ...Love

Residue #103
To the one that wants my soul More than my
body
I will create a life for

Residue #828
You do things to make sure your kids believe
in santa claus
Make sure you do things to make sure that
they believe in themselves
As well

Residue #708
It's not that they fear our empty hands
Or unarmed bodies
They fear our minds, our potential
Our natural universal power
See His'story could only last for so long
Scriptures could make our logical thinking lay
dormant for only so long
Their Whips are now guns...oh but master
Organized united applied knowledge is power
We must realize OurStory
You are not strange fruit...you are the water
and Suns that allowed everything to grow
Don't believe what they told, taught, and
forced upon you
You are Life.. God. Goddess.. Kings..Queens
I believe In the you..that believes in you
All Love..you are not De'feeted ..move

towards elevation.. vibrate high
All energy..positive..awaken..3rd eye..know
self, love self
Respect self, protect self, elect self as owner
of self..
I am

Residue #618
I want to be your life support until you need
life... support

Residue #201
Men
Some women know that they don't have to
F** their way to the top
They simply climb to the top while saying
"F** you kindly, have a nice life"
That ambition, drive, and confidence

Residue #128
Wolves/Dogs use to hunt humans.. Then
they realized
"Hey if we let the humans live, they will hunt
and give us their leftovers and or feed us"
Watch out for those whose ambition is
dormant
You know the coattail riders...waiting on you
to get it and give

Residue #123
A lie doesn't lie

Residue #117

Two things you can do around me
1. Elevate
2. Separate
The first one is your option
The second one is my option
When you're in tune with the universe
Answers to questions that you didn't think
that you had to ask
Will be revealed to you
About things, places, situations, and especially
people
When you're awake.. you see and hear
everything
Even if you don't want to see it
Peep game.. because your success depends on
it
Stay tuned

Residue #1226

I hope you look around at the many things
In your life that were once goals
May they remind you to keep pushing
Inspire you to live with courage and execution
 It can all happen, where there's a will
Will you make it happen

Residue #1224
Wonder what kind of content or substance
would be on facebook
If facebook still required you to have a school
email to sign up

Residue #616
As if my heart needs another scar
You got me stalking falling stars
Just to make a wish

Residue #616-1
Because I don't know when to accept love or
stay friends
I don't know when to let my emotions out or
let love win

Residue #911
Praying that I'm still your weakness when you
grow strong
But if I'm not
At least you'll be strong
And that's all I ever encouraged you to be
Sincerely It's bigger than .....US

Residue #916
I'm missing what I kept missing when all you
asked of me was to listen
I'm reaching for what was within my reach
when your heart was teaching

Unconditional, negotiable, patient ...love
I think back to when you couldn't think back
to a day when
I didn't take your kindness
And pain was the only thing that I could
bring back
And I call myself in love with you
Well I must have fell out
Because I couldn't hear your heart when it
yelled out

Residue #916-1
As flammable as love is...it's so slow to burn
We wrote these chapters yet pages are never
turned
What are we afraid of
Living like strangers as if we've never made
love
Was that love? Or attachment
A crush.. just passion
For the moment.. a time passer by
To me it was love and mine hasn't died

Residue #916-2
Even thou there's a chance that you will treat
me how they treated me
 I'm not going to treat you how I should have
treated them.

Residue #825
Everything that happens
I am to blame, you steal my happiness
Why won't you steal my pain
It could all be so simple
But you'd rather make it hard
The only reason that I'm still single
Is because you're standing on my heart

Residue #720
If I say I love you, I completely do
However, being distant helps the focus
Will do whatever for you at a drop of a dime
Oh youniverse don't let me be misunderstood

Residue # 1014
Put yourself in the mentality that you can't
"Call in"
Because reality is.. it's all on you
Accomplish your goals
Dreamers.. Entrepreneurs

Residue #610
I use to really, really, really want braces, now
I'm cool with my crooked smile
Almost got implants but now I'm cool with
my small breast
Cool with my skinny, lean frame
Shedding a lot of mental skin
Climbing into deeper waters

Realizing that I'm attracted to things that I
never was before
Mostly because of the influence from society,
people, friends
Their opinion of beauty, love, loyalty
I'm super healthy, I'm cool with that
I'm cool to me
Be cool to you

Residue #1012

So thankful that I'm not where I was a year
ago
And where I will be a year from now is far
away from where I am today
Your life is waiting on you, all you have to do
is show up

Residue #5

There is no avoiding love
It can only be postponed
The advantage of your partner's future lover

Residue #825

Don't let a "relationship" dilute
Delay.. destroy.. delete.. diminish..
Defeat...Decrease your goals
You better still do you no matter what
Manipulation of your elevation can lie on the
softest lips...notice the taste it leaves

Residue #1031
You want love that I can't give you and I
blame my ex
The one that came before you and left my
soul a mess
You could be beautiful and the most
deserving
But I need you to know that I'm still hurting
Give me some time
Maybe, my heart will convince my mind
Or maybe my mind will convince my heart
That I should give love a new start
I've never been the one that likes starting over
I search for the sun even when things keep
getting colder
I hold on... I hold on
I hold on
Even when the past becomes so distant that I
no longer know her

Residue #1106
I don't want to be your world...
I want to travel the world with you

Residue #1110
Everything is easier said yet somethings are
never said
Judged my cover but my inner being you
never read

Residue #1002
Some parents don't want their kids to be drug
dealers, hoes, thugs, gay, failures, etc
Do you parents ever think of all of the things
that your kids don't want you to be

Residue #628
I know a lot of talented people whose
challenge is less
 But their environment got them feeling
talentless
Oh boy do I know how friends and family
test
But focus on you and God will manage the
rest
And I hope you manage to see the God in
yourself
During your greatest needs of help
Many accomplishments only require one step
May we all taste and digest our definitions of
success

Residue #325

Inquiring mind: Are you in love

Me: I wish I was

Inquiring mind: Surely you're dating

Me: Not at all.. not even texting

Inquiring mind: You're a great and intellectual person, I find that surprising

Me: I don't like dating.. however, I want my next relationship to last and to be my last

But how do I get there without dating.. humans are difficult

So until then I'm mastering myself.. I love to the soul

Have to make sure that I don't lose myself when that one arrives

Inquiring mind:

Me:

Residue #906

Even a person with alzheimers remembers that they have to eat

You better go get it

Gone Wit It

Residue #513

Is the place you are in life right now different from where you…Ya'll

Were last year

If they're not making you better

Somebody has to be the first to say goodbye

On all ships.. phases and ages

Plateaus and levels

Residue #401

A lot of people are on point and very alert on
April Fool's day
Better be on point every day
Because a lot of people think of you as a fool
every day as it already is

Residue #1216

My most heartbreaking relationship made me
better myself
The "no" from opportunities that I was well
qualified for, made me go harder
The hurtful words and manipulation from
certain family members made me independent
The death of family members and a close
friend make me LIVE
And so on and so on
I go back and look at my facebook post over
the years and see growth mentally and
spiritually Long way to go, yet inspiring to see
the one I have become
Reflect...may everything inspire you to do
better, be better
I DOUBLE DARE YOU TO ALLOW ONE
OF YOUR DEAD LOVED ONES TO
LIVE THRU YOU
Go hard, Live for those who relocated to the

cemetery too soon
DONT DISRESPECT YOUR ABILITIES
You are able and possible
Residue #1220
The only time I get tired...is when I get tired
of You
Then I'll keep it moving.......without......you
Possessing the same drive, same energy, same
focus, same determination, same goals
I owe me and you owe you
Never allow a person to owe you
More than you owe yourself
In reality they don't

Residue #1212
You don't have to die
To rest in peace

Residue #317
It's just better for your peace of mind
Calmness of heart
Strength of focus
Power of energy, and speed of success
If some people hear about you rather than
hear from you

Residue #312
Experience has taught me
Life isn't about giving others a piece of your
mind
 It's more about giving ourselves a peace of
mind Stop reacting
Remove

Residue #323
I'm a sucker for good energy
Motivated by synergy
Inspired by divine alignments and symmetry

Residue #307
God..Universe thank you for the reminders to
put you first, bless the home/mind that I'm in
Bless the homes, minds, hearts of my family
& friends & everyone in between
Thank you for the experiences and truths of
last week, thank you for the food I was able
to Eat least week, goals I accomplished
Thank you for removing unnecessary
thoughts making room for me to have more
positive & productive thoughts today
Thank you for the new cells in my body and
soul
For the pieces that keep me whole when
outside influences attempt to tear me apart.
Bless my closest ones, equipped us with
unselfish yolk so that we may continue to
pour into each other when needed
Thank you for giving us more healthy days
than sick days & more living days than dead
days
If we are holding onto anything that we don't
need, take it from us quickly
For the blessings that we may be looking over
upgrade our vision
Allow our ancestors to be the protectors of
our energy & translators of our intuition

Cover us with light, peace, and love. So shall it be

Residue #305

Soon as I caught wind of Pop Smoke
Sh**, cats can't even win I watched Pop go
Pac said to live and die in La
Nip ain't living, crips cry in La, bloods too
That's what the death of a god'll do
Hustle and motivate help the next over
obstacles
Like you did yourself
But LECK said "If you ever show them the
plug, you just killed yourself"

Residue #317

While you're sitting there
Know that somebody wants your spot
Oh but look at it on the flip side
You might have no other choice but to sit
there
Because somebody already got your spot
Living life is like going grocery shopping
If you go knowing what you want...what you
need
You will save a lot of money and time
What do you want? What do you need
You can have it...trust me...but you have to
GO GET IT

Residue #1120
Someone to bring me pens and blank sheets
When life has given me secrets that I can't
keep
Our room smells like love and power
We get up and shower, whole world feels like
it's ours And we're taking it
No fear.. we're taking it

Residue #1127
Every day you give me lyrics to add to the
song
I'm writing
Even thou I love this song
I hope I never finish it

Residue #323
Diluted frequencies in, makes it hard to sing
see
Turning headphones up distorted sounds
keep the heart off beat
 You keep trying to catch it
Your hooks aren't catchy. pro tools couldn't
edit it
Fear is close to pride so you're also afraid of
open mics
How hard can it be.. how hard is it to say 3
one syllable words
It's just 3 words
You've been feeling them so long that you've
mastered the mix

But when will you let your number one fan
hear it

Residue #1209
It's easy to get caught up in something that's
difficult to get out of
Only let you get to know me slowly because I
don't want the ik to turn into ov

Residue #1214
Depth over distance
Practicing or preparation
You're the perfect image
My Soul's affirmation

Residue #1216
Beautiful intensity fills me with emptiness
I cry with dry tears
I die without fears
As I paint motionless efforts on my lips
"I love you"
And you believe it like the first day that I
exhaled that breath
But today I can't breathe
May I leave

Residue #1223

My lips memorized your goosebumps as if
reading braille
Because you know love can't see
Blind, vulnerable, transparency
Can I rent a room in your eyes
Pay you with affection
And play soft music from my hearts
collection
Spend your nights reading between my thighs

Residue #1225

Only hope knows the disappointment that I
feel
When I look at my phone and it only shows
the time
Knowing that you're responding to everyone's
text but mine
Believed your stories about how your ex
treated you
But if you treated her like you treat me
I think it's her that decided not to be with you

Residue #827

Isn't it crazy how when you feel bad
You can't imagine how it feels to feel good
Then when you feel good you can't imagine
how feeling bad feels

Residue #322

I wonder how the world would be if we

allowed babies
To tell us how life is supposed to be when
they begin talking
If we told them yes more than no, taught
them self-power
And no religions, love and no hate or
aggression
Allowed them to create just allowed them to
be
I mean they are the ones closer to the light
being that they just came from the light Just
because you're the "parent" doesn't mean that
you know it all
Many parents could learn a lot from their
children
Just wondering when the blind will follow
those with vision
When the deaf will listen to the ones with the
message

Residue #909
Many times we love something and want it
until we find out how much it cost
How quickly we change our minds
Yet it's so difficult to apply the same logic
When it comes to loving and wanting
someone
I love my past EX(periences) but I prefer to
waste, lose money
Before wasting time and losing my mind
As I expose my soul, writing songs that u

inspired
Your arms & hands work more muscles
applauding me
Than it took to hold me
As usual you'll get that one day
But I won't wait

Residue #905
Sometime it's God sometime it's YOU
You will know the difference
But when it's YOU AND GOD
YOU'LL tell the difference
"But I've been talking to God for so long
That if you look at my life, I guess he's talking
back"

Residue #831
In a year life went from Depressing me...to
impressing me
I don't go the places that I use to go
I don't know the people that I use to "know"
Back then it hurt me
Now I see that that change was more than
necessary in order for me to Grow
They say don't burn bridges because you
never know when you might need to go back
Well that saying has a lot of people walking
around being fake
If the bridge is shaky, missing a few steps,
charging high "life" tolls
Burn baby burn

Residue #117
Faith without work
Scratches lottery tickets &
Gets back aches from casino chairs

Residue #713
"I know your number by heart"
That phrase associates memory with the heart
Many associate "Love" with the heart
Yet when many fall out of love
They realize that they "thought" they were in
love
I hope I'm explaining my hearts thoughts
simple enough for u to understand
Thinking about changing my name to a seven
digit number
Don't Forget Me

Residue #312
When a dog bites you want to put it down
 But when a horse bucks you off
You want to get back on it
Oh the logic of humans

Residue #310
When you realize a person doesn't need you
Doesn't need to put up with you or do
anything for you
You might appreciate them a little bit more
When you realize that you don't need
anybody

You might accomplish a little bit more
Real-Eyes the balance

Residue #223

He said "that's your family, if you can cut
your family member off, then who am I in
your life?"
 I replied "no,no buddy you should be
questioning why would my family member do
me like that That's why I'll cut them off!"
Only those on a mission can understand

Residue #221

Kids could go far without all of the
manipulation
And lies from their parents or guardians
It produces adults with mental issues
Please break all cycles

Residue #215

Treat me right
Or tell them why I left

Residue #216

Don't pray for me... Envision better days for
me
Envision that I accomplish my goals
Envision my health benefiting me, envision
my mind at peace

Envision my soul reminding me of my
purpose every day
Envision my spirit guiding me
Envision my energy vibrating high
Envision me as the best person that I am
As I will do the same for you
Because if you can see it
You can achieve it

Residue #103
They tell you how to find the Mr. or Mrs.
right
But you don't listen when they tell you
How or when to get rid of Mr. or Mrs. wrong

Residue #205
They want you to live in fear
That's how the top stay at the top
That's why they keep you distracted
Brainwashed...Mindless

Residue #103-1
There are yearbooks stored behind my eye
lids
With water damage from tears that I've hid
But if I let you look into my eyes you will see
no mold
You will only see my soul and all of my truths
that I cannot hold
If I let you
Look into my eyes

Residue #813

There's a difference between loving to try...
and trying to love
But because many love to lie.... we lie to love
We make love believe that we don't want it....
don't need it
Not looking for it... can't receive it.. can't see
it
Can't feel it... even when it's so close that we
can breathe it
We continue to hold our breath.. love
asphyxiation
Eventually you'll say that you miss me
And I'll say I've always been here... you just
missed me
Because there's a difference between loving to
try
And trying to love
We've tried many things....and people
But we never tried to love

Residue #124

You ask how did I lose more weight than I
actually weigh
Because this time I didn't beg her to stay
I threw up all of the lies that I had ever ate
Lost my appetite for the things she put on my
plate

Residue #125

Before taking it there with me
Understand that I'm still in therapy
Post-traumatic stress,
My soul is still mad at my ex

Residue #125-1

You're not where I left you, no
You're a little deeper
Mmm
They say finders keeper
And she decided to keep you

Residue #126

You say every time you try to move on
My name pops up on your phone
Every time you try to love
You can't stop thinking about us and what
was
Thought we were soul mates but do souls lie
Because they definitely cry
Mine won't stop crying for you
It's like mine keeps purposely dying for you

Residue #127

Don't forget to throw away the hotel key
I won't forget the way your body fell on me
So that we can do it again
When she ask
I'm just a friend

Residue #128

Baby if you leave it'll be better for you
But best for me

Residue #608

Who's holding you making sure you're doing
what you're supposed to do
Encouraging the most of you
Every goal accomplished toasting for you
Consistency never a ghost to you
Glue soaking where your heart was broken in
two
Only gentle words spoken to you
Arms open for you, giving their soul to you
Shot gun on the road for you
If there's someone that's what I'm hoping
they do
Or they don't deserve to be close to you

Residue #609

It took listening to a song for you to get the
message
All the years and pain we invested

Residue #122
When they said don't save her
I didn't understand it
I saved her
And learned that hero means last victim
standing
Love Regrets

Residue #722
Even thou we've severed all ties you still give
me butterflies

Residue #630
I love you more than you love you
That's the issue
Can't fix us because I'm too busy trying to fix
you
Wish my body did what my lips do or say
Give anything for the strength to leave today
The only thing that matters is your I's
Blinding you from seeing what matters to me

Residue #429
Ever think.....that thing that you're waiting on
Just might be waiting on you
Move ....can't claim to have faith in the most high

When you don't even have faith in self

Residue #429
When the people calling and texting me the
most

Isn't the person that i think about the most
It irritates me. I need to change my outlook
on things

Residue #429
Anything that was a positive, motivating
influence to me
Before I met you
Will be the same positive, motivating
influence
That encourages me to leave you behind
If need be
May your "why's" be greater than any obstacle
Stay focused...Be not dis'tracked

Residue #214
My guitar is covered with dust
Haven't written much, since we broke up
Sleeping in the living room, because I cry in
our bedroom
Forever just came too soon, forever came too
soon
I'm stuck in never
Thinking about forever

Residue #719
Don't let something you've always had
Keep you from having something you've
never had

Residue #905
Believe me when I say that I need something
to believe in
What did I do to deserve this treatment
What you see as strength is really my
weakness
Holding tears is easy when I avoid speaking
Introvert

Residue #626
Guys see Kesi & ask for puppies if she has
some or to breed her with their pitbull
Isn't it ironic how people have high standards
when breeding their dogs
However, when it comes to human "Mating"
Some have low standards, NO pride of
bloodlines, etc
Asking if Kesi has her shots
Do u have yours
Learn the Science of Mating
Just because you live in America doesn't mean
that you can't create a Dynasty

Residue #601
I think that you just might be my soulmate
No one has ever noticed that I have freckles

Residue #112
Deep in thought I explore
What made you walk out the door
What's deep in my heart I ignore
Because my mind can't take anymore
Happiness and my flesh break up
Pain and my soul make love
Conceiving this intimate state of depression
Believing I could have waited to learn this
lesson

Residue #724
Cold Sheets
Maybe body heat   Induces sleep
Tired of cold sheets   It bothers me
We don't speak
You act as if
You don't know me
Did I ever know you

Residue #903
I want to love you
I want to trust you
It's just things I've put women through
Would you let me know if karma sent you
I just want to know if karma sent you
I need to know
Did foul sh** in my past
Reason those relationships didn't last
Yea I want to love you

And I want to trust you
But we both know what goes around comes
around
Guess I'm scared to see my own tears coming
down

Residue #322
I can't make you love me
I can only allow you to love me and vice versa
I can care about you but I won't fully love you
Until you tell me to or give me permission to
do so

Residue #121
How do I fall asleep without my favorite
bedtime story
Deprived of what the universe created
exclusively for me
Can't help but to feel like I was sent to you
and you to me
To do the things the others never succeeded
to
Too good to be true
So we.. you surrender to fear
Ignoring the fact that I'm here
Willing to protect you before saving myself
Entertaining hopes.. am I playing myself

Playing you over and over and over and over
and over in my mind
Can't seem to get over you

Residue #927
No, I don't have a new number, I have a new
mind
Most of you are in a slumber, wasting time
Sometimes you have to look in the mirror
To help you see things clearer
Looking pass the toothpaste scum, you'll see
you've been paid crumbs
Beating on your chest like king kong
Conversations with you start sounding like
MLK poems
I have a dream
I have a dream
I have a dream

Residue #719
You are the gift and curse Disease and cure
For my ADHD
I focus on you

Residue #1008
You drown me like a hurricane
Shake me like an earthquake
With no consideration of the aftershock

Residue #406

Do you think that you attracted me into your
life or I attracted you into my life
Or was it mutual or just God's goal
If we believe in reincarnation or karmic cycles
Do I feel familiar to you
I sometimes wonder what exactly is this
alignment
The chemistry, the twin flame.. not flame
The oneness of our bodies
I debate if I messed up with you in a past life
and back in your life now to make it right
Or if I promised to always love, protect you
and be there for you in our past life
Evolved through realms, dimensions,
vortexes, hells and heavens
To find you in this life time so that I could
keep my promise
Or I could not question it
But if this something can be perfect
I'd rather know my responsibility

Residue #1993

Been f***ing since I was seven
At family functions around him acting like I
don't remember
Like he isn't the reason my hearts December
towards n***
Don't want them touching me
Don't want them looking at me
That's why I wear my clothes baggy

Residue #319

People don't really f** with you how you
expect
That's why you rarely get pregnant with
success
Have to meditate, ARTificially inseminate
And when you birth the fruits of your labor
they want to claim the kid now
Saying all they did now
But with your morning sickness and expenses
they did no sharing
Heard it was hard for a single parent
But never impossible so always remember
that you're unstoppable
Babymama

Residue #2017

I fell in love with your heartbeat
But you didn't give me the shine that the
other stars see
Gave you thornless roses, watched you leave
And you still can't tell me where it stemmed
from
Striking different poses without me where
you get that film from
This is not how we said we'd develop

Residue #302

There are hearts laying in beds staring at open doors waiting on closure
But I didn't cum to you looking for love and I told you
So let accountability hold you
Between your sheets infused with my scent
Hide your phone under your pillow regretting the last 13 text that you sent
Because I read and never reply
So you hide my alerts hoping the truth is a lie, too infatuated to block me
 Baby, I break hearts
I'm not sure which one of your lips made you believe that you could stop me

Residue #212

You've shown me where wish filled, fallen stars meet
As our souls dance
I appreciate the chance
To allow you the feeling of my heartbeat

Residue #813

There's a difference between struggling and getting back on your feet
A time difference
Some struggle their whole life, that's a mind settling

If you had it before it won't take you long to
get it again
That's a mindset

Residue #817
I was 15 in Sulphur springs
Witnessed moma birth a young king
Something about you made my heart sing
 Something about you I knew you would be
different
Sh** possibly knew you'd be just like me

Residue #810
I be thinking
Come on Tee you're too intelligent to move
this slow
Too old to be broke
Always the one left hanging giving others too
much rope
You can walk on water yet you've been
humble in the same boat
Year after year
Tear after tear

Residue #520
It amazes me how so many have the great
"ability" of "knowing"
A person just by how they dress "he's GAY!"
Or "she's GAY"
Yet the same "life readers" voluntarily and

repeatedly
Hang around liars, fakes, messy people, etc
And don't know, ignore, or pretend not to
know that person is a fraud
Character means more to me than sexuality
Selective vision I guess

Residue #225
A year ago you died tomorrow
Feeling alone I needed a loan
Praying to god asking if he had some time
I could borrow Letter to my granddad
Breathing for those who can't
Living for those who ain't

Residue #804
Guess because since I'm not there
You think that you can just get to me later
Look I know what I bring to the table
But I have never been a waiter

Residue #823
When "she" and "her" are mentioned in the
bible
They're called "wisdom"

Residue #918
I need glasses
But I can see clearly when things need to
change around me and in me

I'm not afraid to break cycles
When I transition from this world
Whatever day it may be
I will be happy, free and at peace
With my life

Residue #811
If only you had invested money
When I hustled for free
Today you wouldn't be charged a fee

Residue #808
Are we loving unconditionally or is this
codependency
Are we what's meant to be or are you trying
to make sense of me
Until.... someone else replaces the scent of me
Somewhere in between potential and
accidental
Purpose and is this worth it
A person can mean the world to you
Yet the world could never equate to that
person
I smile you smile and I'm hoping neither one
of us is silently hurting
Still privately searching for that person
Of a later date
Indecisiveness turn hearts into paper weights

Residue #731
We can do what we do
But don't get caught up in me
Because I'm not getting caught up in you
Unless we have that conversation
If there's no conversations
I'll leave you with your imagination

Residue #730
Use to give me butterflies
Now all you attract is flies, lies
 You know it's me this poetry
When your tomato sauce is poured
Make you eat them words

Residue #723
When you were in town
I found out through instagram
Flexing in my city
Guess you're really not f***ing with me

Residue #705
Biting my tongue isn't as sexy as you biting
my lip
So maybe one day I'll let my emotions slip

Residue #1212
Let you lie to me I love you so I don't care
When she hurts you I let you cry to me I'm
right there

Residue #625

Moma didn't know no better so daddy didn't have to show no better
Still expect child to grow more better
Raised by rnb, and hip hop, but it's like blues was their favorite genre
Moma's tears sung as daddy beat on her
Is this what I have to look forward to
Is this what I was aborted to
This can't be life.. love them both so I can't decide
Can't pick sides with their blood intertwined into mine

Residue #626

I say what I feel and you feel what you don't say

Residue #101

We must first prove to ourselves
Everyone else is secondary
Once WE know, they will know
Whether acknowledged or not
It cannot be denied

Residue #616

We're trying to heal by spraying water on the leaves
When we need to be spraying water on the roots

Residue #611
We only do it when you're under the influence
Whole time I be thinking what are we doing
But I never say no
Because your body touches my soul

Residue #527
Such interesting views from the other side of the table

Residue #527-1
I hope you end your search for love the next time you feel my hug
I'm tired of compromising and bartering
You keep me on the low in your life like I'm a bargain
Probably the richest you ever had
Better than any woman you've ever had
Mentally and spiritually

Residue #728
I feel great!! I wish that I could put this feeling in a capsule
And write some prescriptions
Since I can't I'll just offer some instructions
#1. Focus on you
#2. Focus on you
#3. Focus on you

Residue #522

You disappeared again
I'm not impressed
You're such a predictable magician

Residue #810

My brother told me if they act simple
Treat them simple
You had me running around the A like the @
symbol
I wanted more for us
A lil girl or lil boy for us
But you couldn't pass up them hoes for us
Guess that's just the way love goes for us
Paved two different roads for us
Crushed me on a Wednesday, Thursday we
were a throwback
Listening to what your friends say
Now you wishing we could go back
Wanted to build with you but you couldn't
find structure
Wanted to heal with you
But you rather suffer
Despite what I use to feel with you
I think it's better if you find another
But I doubt you find another ... better
My energy is from a higher power
These other women sipping 5 hour
That's why you always crash
Nothing ever last

Because when it was time to pay attention you
only paid half
But baby don't think too hard you'll be mad at
god
Correct your flaws, avoid self-sabotage
When a goddess lets you beyond her walls
Passed her guards, love yours, and love hard

Residue #1103
You have to pay attention to what you do that
gets you excited
Because the opposite of that causes the
opposite of that

Residue #520
She be water yet one doesn't need to focus on
being a good swimmer
Moreso a good surfer
Ride her waves, predict her tides
When the moon changes its light
Exposing deeper views of the galaxy
Just admire don't become a casualty of the
gravity
Cancer woman

Residue #508

My mind has stopped thinking about you
My heart doesn't even beat around you
My feet are getting tired of taking steps
My soul has stop searching for anything left
Your type of L.o.v.e
Leaves One Very Empty

Residue #506

Rumble young woman it's time to rumble
God said you've been too humble
God said he's sent you many blessings and
you just let others take them from you
God said it's time to firmly plant your feet so
that you can stop stumbling
Speak up and stop that mumbling you have a
voice
You have a choice

Residue #430

Always trust that I'm going to look out for
you
Llike they should have looked out for me
I'm going to support you like they should
have supported me
Love you, learn you, protect you, build you
Grow with you, committed to succeed with
you I
'll always treat you how I'd like to be treated,
deserve to be treated and appreciated

Residue #427
I wonder how I would love how you love
before the heartbreaks
Before the tears filled wells before the fears
and yells
Before the manipulation and abandonment
before the damage meant
No more chances given
Knowing that we should, we still keep our
ability to change hidden
Blame it on the ex why we can only offer pain
to the next
Blame it on the ex why we only expect pain
from the next
Instead we should give credit to the ex for
showing us what love is
And what love is not
So even when we find the one
We keep our hands hidden refusing to grab a
hold

Residue #422
If I wasn't in your life you wouldn't have
anything to cry about
I wouldn't have anything to write about
I turn the the pain into a benefit
But you're getting tired of my bulls***

Residue #1002
W.O.L.F
We Only Love Family Rest in Paradise,
Paradise

LECK letter #952010
"I feel that these misfortunes have come
about for a reason.
For me to learn from them, which I have and
maybe there's someone
I'm supposed to meet or another mental
plateau I have to yet to reach
Then you tell me you will be done in May
Well you can expect me home June or July
(DO NOT tell anyone when I'll be home. No
one knows except you & mom. You should
feel privileged)
Maybe God knew that you would need that
time you spend at school to exert into OUR
grind And of course your credentials won't
hurt either
Plus if we decide to move, I'm ready when
you are
Through our positive energy & our
overbearing desire for the life we are pursuing
We are aiding the universe/god/ ether/world,
to align things in our favor
WE CAN NOT LOSE. It's f***
IMPOSSIBLE!"

LECK letter #8122008
"It really means a lot to hear you like my
sh**"

Residue #420

I don't know what my last facebook post or
Instagram post will be
But I'll always make sure my last words to you
are "I love you"

Residue #416

You use to be my language the only tongue
I could speak
Once was my medicine but now you're the
disease

Residue #414

Immerse me in your water
I give you my air
Cancer Gemini

Feelings #817

Ex left your heart an orphan
How long I waited for it to be up for
adoption
To finally hear that y'all were divorcing
You knew I'd place the highest bid
Once your affection was auctioned
I focused on loving you
You focused on someone who never did
I guarded your insecurities
Removed my impurities

Residue #408
Finally lost the need
To keep your picture up
Finally washed the sheets
Soaked with the scent of us
Did I hold on for too long
Or did you let go too fast

Residue #309
Maybe my move was premature
Maybe I should have gave you another year

Residue #522
I'm supposed to be writing songs
But my pen only writes your name
Deleted your pictures out of my phone
Rejecting calls trying to accept the change
Off.. on.. off.. on..
Here... gone.. here.. gone
Right.. wrong.. right.. wrong
Child... Grown... child.. Grown
You never know what you want
To be

Residue #1127
Every day you give me lyrics to add to the
song
I'm writing
Even thou I love this song
I hope I never finish it

Residue #1217

The way that I love you could be considered
old fashion
But I've been told too many times that good
things die young
I'm wise enough to know that your presence
is something
That I never want to be banned from
When we lay, time stands.. still
Your body temperature is passion, you give
me chills
You f** my mind and thoughts cum
My blood runs
Rivers from my heart into my
tongue's.....Damn
I love you
The way that I love you is frowned upon in
today's society
I go deep within me to give you the highest
me
I look Past my Future to give you the
brightest me
And as I fall for you every day
I hope you notice the
Flyest me

Residue #1996

I remember our conversations like their 90's
rnb lyrics

Residue #1124

I don't know which one I dislike the most
Waking up without you next to me
Or going to bed the same

Residue #1106

I don't want to be your world
I want to travel the world with you

Residue #422

I write as if the paper is god's ears

Residue #1014

Rain, I see that you were trying everything to
drown my positivity
But how quickly you forget I'm indian
I dance for you
So that you can wash that which is not
needed away

Residue #1118

At the moment my heart is everywhere
And my lungs struggle to free the carbon
monoxide from my inside
Inhale..inhale...toxicity on the rise
Organs fail just in time, out of my mind or
out of yours
Is it possible the way that I love music is
equal to how you claim to love me
Well baby runaway, please, because your love
is way too deep
Music and I are already married

Residue #PTSD
And so when I moved back to Texas, my
anxiety was my spouse
I woke up with anxiety, anxiety ate me while I
starved, anxiety lived in me while I was barely
living Dis-ease had taken over my body
I lost weight, I lost confidence, I lost focus, I
lost my vision
My whole life I had been unstoppable
Now I didn't even know where to start
When I say unstoppable
I mean not my family, not a relationship, not
a hater. Not a job, not school
Nothing had ever stopped me from doing
what I wanted to do
When I wanted to do it...how I wanted to do
it, where I wanted to do it
Unstoppable
I looked in the mirror
My eyes were distant and I realized
It was me that was stopping me

Residue #1023
Just thinking......I shouldn't have had to get
that call
I shouldn't have had to ride down those back
roads
With my head out the window trying to catch
the scent of death
Or looking in the sky for birds circling
I shouldn't be out here taking things into my
own hands solving a murder case

Leck and I linked up to do good
While others were linking up to do bad
I have discovered strength in the weakest
places
I don't get tired
Love conquers all
I am the light exposing what was done in the
dark
I can't and I refuse to live with his case being
titled "unsolved" or "cold

Residue #712
Damn wishing I could hit reverse
I would have scooped Leck up he wouldn't be
in no hearse
Killed my boy over what was in his pocket
Yea you got the money but tell me who was
the prophet

Residue #719
I make it so easy to love me. ..but you don't
You make it hard as hell to love you. ..yet I do
What does that say about me
What does that say about you

Residue #823
So many people be holding out on
relationships
Not wanting to give the broken pieces and
unhealed wounds to the next
But when you're healed
You become even more protective of your
scars

Residue #819

I can't decide if I want your soul to leave and
your body to stay
Or your soul to stay when your body leaves
If only my pillow breathed
These walls be talking and their voice sounds
just like yours
Or am I hallucinating, imagining us making
love when I'm masturbating
If only the corners of my sheets could cuddle
Even thou the rim of this wine glass isn't as
soft as your lips
I kiss it over and over believing that e
Eventually this pink wine will taste just like
you in a minute
But the more intoxicated I become the more
I realize that you said what you said and you
meant it

Residue #624

It's hard trying to surprise you with things
Nothing ever seems good enough
And then god asked me
"Did I not make you good enough?"
Did he?

Residue #318
Maybe, I lost my brother at the right time
Maybe, because I've been really on my grind
If everything happens for a reason
He taught me everything needed for achievement
It's been 4 years since I lost my brother and I'm still hurting
Maybe tears are still swirling because they say he deserved it
How.. how.. how
And I can hear him saying
"Tee you ain't got to explain sh** to these mulf**s
Get buried 6ft and you'll see how much they really love you"

Residue #1108
If god asked you who or what I am to you
What would you say?

Residue #1013
Beliefs can be manipulated and or destroyed
So I live by what I know

Residue #117
Jobs are more likely to give you a day off for a relatives funeral
Before they give you a day off for a family reunion
Why? Mmm maybe because they know they are guilty of over working & under paying you

To the point that you can't even afford a
family reunion
That doesn't sting as much as
Not Being able to afford to attend a relatives
funeral
Programming slaves to put unimportant
things above the most valuable things
We talk to fake "friends" more than family
Wreck brains to cut thoughts down enough to
fit inside of tweets & facebook post
Before calling relatives just to say 3 WORDS..
8 LETTERS
This Earth we live in... die in
Reach out to your relatives today
Exchange some life stories with them..
especially the elders
Emotion city

Residue #123
Harriet Tubman called wondering why no
one ever spoke of "Whip" control
Sadly, I didn't have an answer
Then my great-great-great-great grandfather
called asking why
People didn't create a fuss about "Rope"
control
After seeing him swaying in the wind like
strange fruit
And again I... had no answer

Residue #1223
You asked how I'm doing, I replied "getting
closer to my dreams"

However, I leave out the distance
Because I don't need you treating me
different
Quick to ask to come back stage
Making me feel that our friendship is
something that I need to reevaluate

Residue #1213
Never disrespect your ex by getting with
someone that's not above their level
If you settle for less...then what was the point
of leaving
Or maybe that's why they left you

Residue #730
Many days I wish my moms had a different
childhood

Residue #728
How many times have you said R.I.P (insert
names here)
And you still choose to be stuck in your ways
If it can happen around you
It can happen to you
Release selfish ways and thoughts

Residue #709
When you give someone a ride on a very hot
day
And the AC in their car doesn't work
But they roll their window down while your
cool AC is blowing

Some people just want to feel the same. ...and stay the same

Residue #513
People come and go
Opportunities sometimes just
Go

Residue #502
Jobs have turned "starving" artists into "WAITING" artists
Waiting to save money for studio time
Waiting to save money to relocate
Waiting to get shows, waiting to do this, waiting to do that
Waiting for the right time
Waiting, waiting and more waiting

Residue #107
In the days where people are willing to ride and die
For those that they don't know
While murder cases in their own towns turn cold

Residue #321
Emotion filled text Deleted
Never sent

Residue #1223
I don't have kids because I'm Selfish
Nawl I don't have kids because I feel helpless
I won't bring a child into this system
That was written to make them victims
They'd for sure kill mine, my son would be
Tupac in the flesh
Daughter would be Harriet reincarnated ready
to free the rest
Shotgun to every race back, let's not turn
back, as if we ever really got ahead
Needed leaders but being a leader got them
dead
So now many won't speak up, praying on
their knees, but never pick their feet up
Take one step, they say he'll take two
I apologize to my never to be born child
But moma will let them kill me
Before I let them kill you

Residue #1218
If you can remember who introduced you to
Fear
Then you will remember where you left your
POWER

Residue #1203
You are the constant object of my thoughts
My imagination exhaust itself in guessing
what you are doing
I only find comfort in knowing that you can't
replace me
Boomerang

Residue #507

Hold on to your heart today
Hold on to your heart today
Don't fall apart today
How many times did I have to say that in the
mirror
Heart gets colder, soul darker when my eyes
tear up
And I keep taking pain I keep taking pain
slow
Find the innerG spiritually I learn to grow
They try to tell me hold on god'll make it right
But can I cry tonight can I cry tonight
Because my brother got kidnapped and then
he died that night
And I've been having murder fantasies
Seeing Family and friends as enemies
I be glad when they catch them man
Beacause if I ever ever catch them Man
I'ma kill em
Hold on to your heart today
Don't fall apart today

Residue #1029

Why are you complaining
Back and forth, so draining
Do you see what I'm saying
Love is decaying
Let me really know what you got going on

You act like I'm the one who did you so
wrong
Late night face time
Proving I'm home
This isn't the past time
Like the last time
You might be better off alone
You finally found something that's real
But you still need some time to heal

Residue #1214
Sun peeking thru my blinds
Arm reaching but can't find You
Then you appear in my memory
Bury myself in these sheets
To feel you in dreams
Past betrayed the future
Present

Residue #1007
Damn they did the dead wrong, my head
gone
Too many n*** names on headstones, the
feds home
To my n*** who got bread wrong, or got
snitched on
Brought the wrong b*** home now he got
kids home
That these streets are going to raise, that these

streets are going to play
That these streets are going to grave
You figure if they had a father figure these
n*** in these streets would be saved
Paved concrete covered with graffiti like
hieroglyphics in the tomb of Nefertiti
 New rituals being displayed for the new...
slaves

Residue #1219
If my dreams never come true
I'll be satisfied with sharing reality with you
All we had in common was pain
Same characters, new names
I think I've found that thing that Romeo died
for
You've got a heart my heart cries for
Baby can I love you honestly
Can I love you perfectly

Residue #1015
I still make breakfast for 2
Guess my right mind left with you
Making up the bed my tears kiss the sheets
I remember when you said you'd leave

Residue #1022
Liars will never fess up
They're just messengers
Flesh is testable
That's what lessons are for
I love Aaliyah but there's no back and forth
Flipping the re-up
To get what we've never had before

Residue #1124
Can you come over
And make me come over And over
Again

Residue #426
I knew you still kinda had feelings for your ex
And was afraid to give your heart to the next
I did my best to be worth it to you
I remember nights I slept at your house, I'd
stay up all night
Because I didn't know if I was a snorer and I
didn't want you to hear me snoring
I wanted to be perfect to you
Been told heaven is beyond the sky
I wanted to earth it to you
Conceive loves last child and birth it to you
I wanted two... of you
Or maybe 3, 4,5,6 or 7 billion of you because
to me you're all that this world needs
All that I need in the form of flesh
And telling you my deepest feelings I mostly
procrastinate

But there's no urgency for me to be your girl
When I already know that you're my soulmate
I'm gone baby, gone baby but I won't be long
You know I gots to get my hustle on

Residue #616
Recognize and Appreciate the ones that go all
in with you
You know the ones that roll with you until
the wheels fall off
Not the ones that keep you spinning your
wheels

Residue #630
A friend of mine dog was going after
someone
And my friend grabbed his dog to stop him
 His dog turned and bit him on the shoulder
My friend put a bullet in his own dog on the
spot
Now I don't know how bad Kesi would have
to bite me for me to shoot her
But it made me think
How many times we let humans bite us
Mentally, physically, spiritually, etc
And we let them over and over
Sometimes because of love and or attachment
Nowadays you have one time to bite me

Residue #1013

When I turned 10, my dad use to wake me up
Early on the weekend and summertime
I would say "Why do I have to get up, there's nothing to do"
He replied "Find something to do!"
He had me out mowing yards
Daddy made me a hustler

Residue #921

Leck really taught me what "keeping a name alive" really means
Seeing his pain of losing Trae
The events he held for him, the lyrics he wrote about him
 "Clicked up with Trae, and we just rapped about our real life
 When you died for a second, I didn't want to feel life
I didn't want to feel nothing sitting here in all white
All I felt was Moma's hand Jr it will be alright
NO IT WON'T cause yal leaving and I got to stay the night
It's f** up feeling like your lucks up, and it's done ran out
And everything you planned in for in life, it never panned out"
I felt the same when they murdered T-Dub aka Leck Thinking
Damn what a cycle

Residue #1210
_____ my way to the top
Because a lot of people are _____ for a lot
less
Some for nothing

Residue #1112
At a certain age it would be wise to realize
that it's not wealthy or healthy
To point the blame at others for your poor
emotions, sadness, stress, etc
Pity parties are cool once a week but not
every morning, afternoon, evening and night
Getting defensive during general
conversations isn't cool
What everyone says isn't directed towards you
but if the shoe fits
Acknowledge, observe, change for the better
We must grow, we must know
Grow yourself or sit your frustrated,
depressed, stressed butt in a stagnant porta
potty
The whole world isn't against you, sometimes
you're against yourself
Vibrate higher. living that triple A life around
here
Awake, Alive, and Able
Know yourself and not that BS that you have
been told and conditioned to believe
Your body is equipped with everything
needed to heal itself
The soul is equipped with everything to

elevate itself
Find the Hid'story

Residue #918

A lot of parents be acting
They don't really do as much for their kids as
they tell the world they do
Public success, private failures
The position your child could be in with just a
little of your support
Universe bless the child that gets their own
Break a cycle, transform future generations

Residue #1205

Sometimes I feel that I cry too much
Then I realize not all of the tears are mine
I try to constrain myself when it seems like
I'm fighting too much
But a lot of the fight isn't all mine
I cry for you, I fight for you, I stand for you
All minds will eventually have peace
Hearts will mend a little and chapters will
meet closure
Mothers of the unsolved murder victims

Residue #1215

People will get fighting mad at you for
wanting better out of them
Before they get mad at themselves for not
doing better
Third eye see the god in you
Continue to appear as a myth

Or show them why they should believe in you
It's your choice
I'm just a profit, and I do mean profit

Residue #1101
Did the thought of them make you question
the point of living
Did the thought of them keep you up at night
as if your body never knew what sleep was
Did the thought of them make you lose your
appetite for weeks
Did the thought of them break the levees in
your eyes
Did the thought of them destroy your trust
Did the thought of them make you feel like
your future would be insufficient
I just want to know what exactly brought you
to the conclusion that they didn't deserve to
live See you can go see who you love, hug
who you love
Text who you love, call who you love, tell
who you love that you love them
We can't
Maybe if I try to show you where we're
coming from
You will understand WHY WE ARE
COMING SO HARD

Residue #1127
It's thanksgiving
Looking at your obituary
No thanks given
Christmas is next and I just want one present
I just want you present

Residue #1002
I detoxed, and all night I dreamed of you
Guess I wasn't as clean of you, as I seem to
you
Because I don't talk to you, won't walk to you
What you took from me doesn't compare to
what I brought to you
Stole what you wanted, neglected what you
needed
Has to be haunting, that I'm the one who
succeeded

Residue #524
Exist in the world
But don't let the world exist in you

Residue #1209
All of us are self-made
But only the successful ones will admit it

Residue #2016
Imagine your sentence
If you premeditated your success
Law of attraction
Whatever you see you manifest

Subconscious mind is never at rest
Make sure your next thought is your best

Residue #1210
Don't get mad at others when you
Told you, "NO" first
You can have whatever you put your
subconscious mind to

Residue #512
You think my feelings are too strong
I think you lead me on
Now we're sitting here saying goodbye
And I feel the sun is falling out of the sky
I'm trying to figure out how to walk away
I never prepared for this day
Because now we're sitting here saying
goodbye
And I feel the sun is falling out of the sky
Erased your number out of my phone
To make sure I don't call when I'm alone
Because we sat there and said goodbye
And I watched the sun fall out of the sky
I'm trying to walk away
But I can't
Thought I'd be ok
But I ain't
Because we sat there and said goodbye
And I watched the sun fall out of the sky

Residue #619

As I travel to the place that they call sleep
A million emotions attack me
What-ifs and the could-bes
If you were still here with me
No matter how hard I try to move on
The love for you is still strong
I don't know how long it's going to take
For you to be forever erased
Out of my mind, out of my thoughts
Take my pain, memories get lost
Out of my mind, away from my heart
Off my time, you're tearing me apart
Love, I'm missing you
But love at the same time I'm dissing you
Because I know that you're not worth it

Residue #2007

T.I said be 21 about the situation
Whether you're quiet or spitting
Standing or sitting
They're still hating
I'm confused I don't know how I'm supposed
to feel
Running through life but it's nothing when
you're living on a treadmill
I take my steps, control my breaths
What I thought was right turned out and left
And what I felt, giving no help, left with
welps
All by myself
It's a feeling in my stomach that makes me
want to throw up

But there's nothing to keep me from it
So I guess I have to grow up

Residue #1125
Observing how they rewrite history so
generations stay lost and confused
You will remember Isis for being a terrorist
group
Not an Egyptian Goddess

Residue #1123
Many will text "LOL" and they don't laugh
out loud
They will say "praying for you" and don't
pray for you
They just talk about your situation
Beware of the energy you invite

Residue #030
I thought I had it made, started running the
same plays
Until you knocked me off my dribble
I tried to pivot and go the other way, but
there was nowhere to go
No one to pass the blame
Only option is to carry myself
Heart left with a crucial sprain
With only seconds left
I worked my ass off to make it to the play
offs
One cross over cost me the game
I need braces to support my legs because I'm
falling

My shoe strings wouldn't stay and I kept
tripping
I jump to block your words and you say I'm
fouling
I brought the streets to home court wilding
Now I'm on defense watching someone else
Take advantage of my careless turn over
And the crowd is cheering her on
But I'm hustling trying to get back in my zone
I know I hurt you but please don't hurt me
I'll do what I have to do just don't retire my
jersey

Residue #311

I don't know what kept my faith in believing
That you could ever love me
Because everything you ever showed me
Proved that you wasn't thinking of me
Wasted years
So many tears
My biggest fear was seeing you disappear
I'm stronger now
I'm done now
So numb now
I'm running out
I'm leaving
Your cheating almost stopped my breathing
But my heart is still
It's still beating it's still beating
Your name pops up on my phone and I just
let it ring

No I don't want to be alone but I can't let you
keep hurting me
I need to pick up my things from your place
But I'm afraid face to face that you'll convince
me to stay
I don't want to
I can't
So don't ask me
Because I'm not going to stay

Residue #606
I remember looking out for you when I didn't
have to
I remember reaching out to you when I didn't
have food
 I remember you didn't do because you didn't
have to
What if I had hit you with that same attitude

Residue #1102
When it was time for the game
Who was you rooting for
When them n*** came
Who was you shooting for
Riot in my life
You looted more
Whole heartedly blessed you
With things you weren't suited for

Residue #1221

It's been like four years and
You're coming out of your coma
My eyes fill with tears because
I don't know if I really want you
Breathing on our own
It's only when you're weak that
I am strong
I pray the wires stay plugged up
Because I don't want to lose your love
You can walk baby
But please don't leave me behind
If you want to talk baby
Use my mind
Because if you wake up baby
I'll flatline
Because if you wake up baby
I'll flatline
Family and friends saying you will make it
But what about me
I don't think that I can take it
So many times I said I'll change
Turn right back around
And did the same things
Forgive me forgive me, for being selfish
But I love you and I can't help it

Residue #430
Nowadays while counting the funds that's
kept on me
I remember days counting the ones that slept
on me
Blood of my blood flesh of my flesh phony
Never showed love never wished the best for
me
Me and my granny don't get along
But she always said god had a test for me
I had just left home got the call that they
killed my best homie
Lonely on top of lonely
Feeling like the whole world owes me
Forced me to be the woman my moms never
showed me

Residue #831
She didn't get the part
Skin too dark
Hair too thick
Breast too small

Residue #503
I was praying to god while others disobeyed
him
Leck was praying to god too but it seems like
god betrayed him
After three weeks of searching they finally laid
him
Under a f***ng bridge where the animals
could graze him

I got the suspect names and addresses of who
raised them
I don't know if hell exist but god ain't going
to saved them
 When I run up on them mul***s and repay
them
With an urn their families can place them
They took away a real one
When they should have took the ways of a
real one
In his own lane, getting his own sh**
They say the streets is to blame
I say he was f**ing the wrong b**
Little did she know killing him would hurt the
wrong b**
I'm on her couch with her kids like "welcome
home b**"
Which one do you love the most? Which one
do you want to live
When murder hits close, it destroys all fears

Residue #715
Said that they got me but never did they get
me
Who was there to spot me
Whenever I was lifting
Seems they forgot me when things started
shifting
Thought it was us against the world
Until you turned against me

Residue #1029
I said things you said things that we can't take
back
Is this a lust thing, love thing
Or are we just attached

Residue #610
Aunt Betty on hospice she don't want to die
alone
I'm on the other side of the phone like damn
I'm going to die alone

Residue #430-1
Told me they found my brother breathless
My mind totally just rejected it
You can tell me every day
But I'll never accept it

Residue #228
Seeming things never go my way
High beams on the highway
Wanting to hop the medium
Heartbroken imagining my brothers having to
talk to mediums
Just to talk to me
I can hear the youngest now like
"Tee how come you didn't talk to me"

Residue #117
My moms is sleep, that keeps me up at night
I hate how she be
But little brother said "sissy we're going be alright"
When I heard that it made me want to fight
She tried to hold us down, haha we reached new heights

Residue #627
Sometimes when I'm around people I have to step away and catch myself
Always been quick on my feet but sometimes tears fall that I can't even catch myself
You caught bullets that I would have tried to catch myself
If I was there
At times it seems like I'm by myself when I look for people who care
Told your mom to just pray and I'll do the rest myself
Told her to rest.. she tells me that I need to rest myself
Your death was out of my control but I feel I could have changed it I can't help myself
I shouldn't have left you I blame myself
Seeking therapy and medication because I'm falling and I can't help myself

Residue #909
Emotions that I feel at night
Let me know wounds ain't healing right With
you I could see past the sky
Now I can't see the ceilings height
All is possible with will and fight

Residue #811
You ask if I ever think about you
To understand the extent it would be better
to ask if I ever stop thinking about you
Maybe I would stop if I allowed someone else
to influence the habit
But I'm afraid that just might be a temporary
solution
Sometimes having nothing is better than a
substitution
Least that what I tell myself when in reality
I just don't want anyone else

Residue #123
I hope you know
That for every tear that falls from your eyes
I cry 3
One for us
One for you
And one for me
When the night comes, I remember your light
Strong armed by bed sheets colder than our
last goodbye
Becoming soggy in hot showers attempting to
wash away memories

Of how lovers....became enemies
I cry
In the presence of butterflies
I acknowledge my broken wings
My inability and all unspoken things
That could have made your song sing
Instead...you cried
Because I...tried...sh**, I tried..Man, I Tried
But since trying is the same as delaying
Your cries kept replaying until one day
I had no excuse for why I wouldn't be staying
Who's lost is it or who's lost,tripping
Over nothing about anything concerning
everything related to nothing
Man that Sh** is NOTHING
Compared to my nervous system when
electrified by your fingerprints
How your voice causes silence to bend
Into high frequency, frequently
Sex screams so intense
You'd think that the twin towers were falling
again
Together we shake nations
That's why my soul committed suicide
Noticing that we went from love making
To hand shaking...to distance
To vacant
I hope you know...that for every tear that falls
from your eyes
I cry 3...

One for Us
One for you
And one for me

Residue #707
Why should I expect a stranger to be a friend
to me
When I got blood that don't even act like
they're kind to me

Residue #701
The ceiling fan circulates the silence
Bringing more awareness to this lonely bed
I'm in
I question perfect timing
Should I be thankful to learn so soon that,
you were lying

Residue #331
Y'all killed a legend
A blessing
How you murderers out there resting
How many times are y'all going to kill god
When he's trying to turn your earth into
heaven
How many times are y'all going to kill OUR
GODS
With THEIR weapons
Hearts full of self hatred
I wish you could love you
Depart from escalations as if your enemy was
you

Let them live.. let us live
Heal.. let us heal
Contrary to belief LOVE does taste better
than tears
Love will strip us of fears
They don't know our pain like you and I do
To hold this pain is to be suicidal
At least one time a day
Despite our efforts, seems opportunities keep
flying away
But the marathon continues

Residue #131
Knew you had 2 different faces
Instagram you got 2 different pages
What you post shows me your heart is in 2
different places
Which one is facts
Which one is just for the likes
If your trying to save your past
Why are we spending this time

Residue #913
When her ex tried to fight her
She saw my ambition as a rider
It ain't no question where my heart be
F** with her it'll be a gangsta party
For me she'll do the same

Done shed so many tears but with me there's
no more pain
If b**es got all eyes on me she'll bomb first
Her soul is all I need she comes first
They might have the will but ain't no way
Any of these actors can take my Jada from me
When I come home from running the streets
She knows only god can judge me
I ain't mad at ya, unconditional love
I get around getting this bread up
In this white mans world she say baby keep ya
head up
What I do for love
And all she has to do is smile for me
Thug passion, how do you want it baby

Residue #006
He said "come here little girl let me show you
a secret"
Then he made me promise to keep it
He said "take this and lick it like a lollipop
Be quiet because if your parents hear we will
have to stop"
He gently touched me like he loved me
Trusting him I let him climb on top of me
It was my first time so it hurt like hell
He whispered in my ear "Don't tell"
He kissed my neck as he tried to slide in
I said "stop" but eventually he went right in
He held my hands down and started out slow
Before I knew it my P*** swallowed his D***
whole

It was the worst pain in the world
Because I was only 6 years old

Residue #310
I've seen you without make up
Seen how you are after a break up
How mean you become all the things that you
make up
Fragile on the inside but try to play tough

Residue #301
Has anyone's energy ever just left you feeling
healed
Diminished your anxiety, settled your
stomach, and drove away the chills
Has anyone ever aligned the chakras of your
soul
Allowed your energy to freely flow
Because they see that you're worth your
weight in gold
Has anyone ever just wanted to play you
music instead of playing you
And when asked who's the most important
girl in this world
They end up saying "You"
You purchased all of the real estate in my
state of consciousness
And although my admiration for you wished
to stay anonymous
It's difficult when you manage to stay
beautiful even when things are ugly around
you

I'm glad others lost you and I found you
Sometimes love is a gym membership with a
complicated cancellation policy
Still I can't stop myself from giving you all of
me
I pray that you use my loyalty and consistency
as the tracking number for our ships'meant
To relate our hearts minds, and souls
Trusting each other with parts we've never
shown
So when the world refuses to admit it
We can lift each other's heads up knowing
how much we've grown
I'll be the organic food for your thoughts
To help you avoid the greatest lesson ever
taught
Not being prepared for opportunities
I want success more for you than me
I'm here to assist your spiritual, your mental,
your emotional healing
The midwife for all of the gifts that god chose
you to birth
And out of all of the world's presents
I'll always choose you first

Residue #127
I'm strong enough to be vulnerable with you
We are what we are
Whatever that is
In parallel dimensions influenced by
Undiscovered frequencies

Residue #102

Excuse me if I chase me
More than I chase you

Residue #1121

I love you in the most healthiest and unselfish
way
I'm willing to be everything and nothing at
the same time
I understand that you still have healing to do
In the meantime
I'm here to show you true love

Residue #207

When you roll up and your eyes are still low
Roll over just to find your pillow
Do you ever just want to feel more
Like my body on top of yours
When the night seems cold and longer
Do you ever want to pick the phone up
And tell me "Baby come on over"
To sit your inner thighs on my shoulders

Residue #81202

See moma didn't raise a fighter
But don't think that she raised a lover
Because if she did maybe
I would love her
Sometimes her actions make me say F** her

Residue #711
I begged you not to leave
You left anyway
Your reason was because I didn't beg you to stay
I asked you to love me
You answered with pain
I wonder how can hurting again
Be associated with a gain

Residue # 910
Wondering home, pondering how both my step grandparents are gone
Is that confirmation of the mistake my grandparents made
When they chose to break up
Grandma says granddaddy lives in his whiskey dreams because he's afraid to wake up
But granddaddy says what she says is really beautified make up, I mean lies
To make him look like a bad man
When all of except two of her kids are by a different man
I don't know who to believe so I just read lips and sip my tea

Residue #313
Tears fall searching for the best well....being
Being lovable doesn't guarantee love

Residue #1023
I'm making promises that I know I can't keep
Just seeing if you'll believe me
I'm drinking water that I said I wouldn't
swallow
Making rules that I know I can't follow
Crying to you but I'm the one suffering
Because I know I could never love you again
I just want to be friends

Residue #813
My neighbor lost her little boy yesterday
Because her best friend got mad called cps
and they took him away
They say her drug and drinking habits aren't
ok
All alone my neighbor committed suicide
today
Because of the recession my cousin can't
afford daycare
But her brother doesn't have a job, he's
always there
He loves spending time with his niece so he
volunteers
When mommy is gone, uncle hugs his niece
and pushes himself inside of her

Residue #1201
What I thought was love is now just writing
material
But I'm not complaining, all of the words you
ignored
I'm about to have the whole world singing

Residue #904

Thought we were going to the ocean
Left me in the desert instead
Thought we were going on vacation
All that was to mess with my head
I thought we were having a good time
Being you and me
Then I woke up to find out
I was just temporary company

Residue #825

I lie awake eyes wide open
I'm tired but I'm fighting sleep hoping
You'd pick up the phone or come over
Because ice is in my bones and my blood is
colder
If pain is love
Please hate me
Hate me enough
To save me
From breaking down
Other day came home and called your name
Convinced I'm all alone because no one came
No eating, sleeping, tv, or phone just crying
Without you here with me I'm slowly dying
If pain is love
Please hate me
Hate me enough
To save me
From breaking down

Residue # 1009

There could be no traffic
The sun can be shining
But it's a habit
I can't be on time when
I need to be at work
And really hurts, what I deserve
Isn't what I earn according to their firm
I'm putting in my 2 week notice
It's time for me to get focused
So that I can get noticed
I'm putting in my 2 week notice
They're telling me my performance is
beginning to suck
Threatening to write me up
But I've just had enough
Yesterday was like today and I know
tomorrow will be the same stuff
Sometimes you're going to want to throw the
towel in
Sitting at work feeling like you're wasting your
talent
One day you're going to say F** it
Finally follow your heart and trust it

Residue #1212

I arrived on the same day as Anne Franklin
When age 5 hit, I was Shaniya Davis except I
survived it
I blame that for all of my failed relationships
Learned early not to trust a man
Years later, I'm with a female walking hand in
hand

Damn.. how do I break this to my parents
But from my style of dress it should be
apparent
Church people keep staring and judging me
Not considering how long this world has
been F**ing me
Sucking me, then they lose F**ing sleep
When I tell them that I'm about to F**ing
leave
Stay? For what?
So that you can sink your claws in deeper into
my tender skin
Remember when you didn't have a pot to piss
in
And everyone acted like it was a lot to listen
To your issues
Ears open, palms full of tissue
I had your back wishing for a b*** to diss you
I've always been a caregiver
Many times it back fired
Because...hurt people hurt people
Yet I've hurt not one so maybe I'm not hurt
just disappointed
By the fact that people's words can be so
double jointed
Two faced, multiple faced
Yet I remain in her face
I'm with her when I don't pick up my phone
And she's with me even thou she tweets how
much she loves being alone She's young and
dumb, I'm wise and grown
But why is it her telling me that it's best if we
both move on

Guess I'm Stevie Wonder when it comes to love
She's lil John she doesn't give a F**
So I run away as fast as I can like Kanye said
Hoping to one day be able to say I'm doing just fine like Wanye said

Residue #1211
I loved you with a love that only someone
Who's committed suicide can relate to
Before and ever since

Residue #1117
Not even god could have predicted
That I'd be this unpredictable
So forgiving yet unforgivable
Really was what I did that critical
That you couldn't look pass my flaws as I did for you
Your lies are for my protection
But my lies require correction

Residue #422
I'm in the studio trying to write some dope sh**
Your moms called me crying your death she can't cope with
I told her it'll get better but really I don't know this
Pain got me feeling kind of hopeless, if I knew where the rope is
I would hang myself
Since you've been gone I hang with myself

Who can I trust, the suspects are the same
ones who use to hang with us
I can't adjust
They're strangers, and I know the more I try
to solve the case
The more they want me lying next to you

Residue #407
Took me a while to see that you were a
parasite in me
Skewed my vision to the point that I saw you
as an organ
Now that you've been removed
I clearly see that you aren't important

Residue #303
If I can't have you to myself
Then I'll settle for your shadow
If I can't have you in the physical
I'll put you in my mental

Residue #408
Q: Would you ever date me
Me: Uh duh but every time I turn around
You're either back with your ex or with
someone new
I'm more than just an option

Residue #205
As children we looked at some adults as
adults
Now as adults we look at those same adults as
children
Childish just childish
However, glancing at the leader
It's easy to see how the generations before us
got their mentalities
Families and their unconscious cult like
tactics.... escape
Sometimes we can hear the wrong thing from
the Right person
We looked up to you, your hands could have
untied the blindfold
If nobody else chose to tell us the truth
You owed us.. owe us truth
But.. hey whatever.. you can have the title but
you have to earn the respect
Family Elders

Residue #1020
And when the hearts stop warring
The mind sometimes still feels the need to
fight
For too many yet no reason at all
Toxic relationship

Residue #611

"The reality of this cold world, it's got my soul hurting
They took Leck too young, he should have been an old person
I'm carrying on new ones, even thou I got my own burdens
Sh**t weighs two tons, got the back of an old person.."
If I could have anything this year.. tomorrow
I'd want another 5 yrs..10 yrs..15 yrs.. with him
If that's too much I'd take another 6 months
I know we would get a lot done
And yea there's nothing we can take to the next life
And all of our accomplishments become memories
But when you have something in common with someone
Interest,faith, goals, drive, determination, craft
All the things that help you keep your head up, that help troubles seem a little smaller
That help stars seem a little closer.. it really makes a difference in living
He helped me dream big, there was never an idea that he said was out of our reach
He would say expand that thought, think deeper
Research and turn one idea into five different business plans
His shoes can never be filled in my life
We thought we had time.. and with so many

goals we knew it would take time
But
If you want.. if you NEED to do something..
Do it. work towards it.. NOW
If you have a friend.. recognize it and be a
friend
They are RARE
They say blood is thicker than water however
some friends are the reason that your cup is
HALF FULL

Residue #1005
Personal diaries come equipped with a lock &
key
A chef won't give you all of his recipes
A songwriter has notebooks of songs and you
will never hear many of them
Listen close to...chew slow on what others
allow you to know
Flip pages without permission
And see how quickly reading the book by its
cover becomes your only option

Residue #908
So you mean to tell me
Your kid can pick his or her own switch for a
whooping
But can't pick the dream that their heart is
telling them that they should be pursuing
We don't need "freedom of Speech" ...we
need "freedom to Be"
Speaking, talking, etc is why many things
haven't and aren't getting done now

No more sheep
protect your Live....Stock
Market that

Residue #823
How you get mad because she let another
man hold your child
When you don't provide food or shelter for
your child
Boy don't you know that you control her
smile
You're responsible for her happiness
Laid down and made her but what's happened
since
That's what I be talking about when I be
talking about you boys not having sense
Got the shoes, the clothes, and the jewels
But check the bank accounts and discover
them boys not having cents
What about your seeds Johnny apple

Residue #817
If only they would rush to upgrade their
mentalities, standards, and energy
Like they upgrade their phone

Residue #1009
Good before I met you F** around and
forget you
Like amnesia

Residue #1217
Your stomach growls a little different
When your funds are insufficient

Residue #418
Some people go to school and do everything
the teachers say
Just to graduate
Some people go to work and do everything
and anything their managers say Just to keep
an overworked underpaid job
But when it comes to some people doing
things for themselves
They hesitate or run for cover
There's a thin line between survival and
slavery
Give me corn, I make corn bread

Residue #1229
I remember your name like it's the password
to survival

Residue #205
Feels like I'm too selfless majority of the time
But if you f*** over me
You f** over god

Residue #427
Some days I really want u
Then there's days that's not true
I've got feelings 4 someone else
Yet I want you both to myself
These are just confessions of a polyamorous
heart

Residue #608
Some people hang around you until they get
what they want
Not realizing with a little more patience and
pure loyalty
They would eventually receive everything they
need

Residue #LecksPoem

Before us..
There was me
And somewhere out there was you
We were hiding from each other in plain sight
Lost in a sea of uncertainty & fear
Afraid of the consequences of chance
Before us, there were my dreams
Dreams of the kind of love that's spoken of &
rarely lived
A love that exists only in the mind of the one
who longs for it
Dreams of a face, featureless, yet angelic in
appearance
An image of perfection that lives forever
within the depths of my subconscious
Before us, we wade's through rivers of
disappointment
Crossed desolate plains of heartbreak
And passed by each other, only to end up in
the midst of pain, searching for hope in a
maze of loneliness
Before us, there was me, then there was you,
then there was me & you
Found by each other destiny & brought
together by the magnetism of our souls
yearning for one another
We are no longer hidden, & have gone from
lost, to finding our way
Dreams of love are becoming a reality & the
subconscious image of my perfect angel
Has gone from a vision only seen by my

mind's eye to a comforting actuality
Disappointment only comes when you don't
& loneliness is only there when you aren't
And heartbreak, what is heartbreak?
It is the very things that has been crushed by
the immensity of our hope for the future
Before us..
Was a time forever lost in memory
Before us..
There was nothing because you are my
everything

Residue #365
I have a chest full of notebooks dating back
to 1995
I didn't squeeze everything into this book
However, I always said that I would release a
poetry book
If not to anyone else
I always keep my word to myself
Another goal completed